LOVE'S DECEPTION

UNTANGLING TOXIC BONDS

Author: S.B

TABLE OF CONTENTS

DEDICATION

To my incredible family and friends, the unwavering pillars of my life, whose love and encouragement have been the light in my darkest moments and the celebration in my brightest. You stood by me through every challenge, lifting me when I stumbled and cheering me on when I found my stride.

To my parents, whose wisdom shaped my character and whose sacrifices taught me the value of perseverance. To my siblings, for their boundless laughter, unwavering honesty, and reminders that even when the world feels heavy, family remains a constant. To my friends, who reminded me, with their late night calls and unshakable faith, that even in my moments of self doubt, I was never truly alone.

This book is not just my story; it is a reflection of the love and belief you've poured into me. For the readers holding these pages, I hope you find echoes of your own strength within the words. May this book serve as a reminder that no matter the storm, there is always a way forward.

Thank you, from the depths of my heart, for being my guiding light.

ACKNOWLEDGMENTS

——————《《 ᘗᘏᘊᘈᘗᘏ 》》——————

This book is not just the result of my efforts but a testament to the collective support, wisdom, and love of so many incredible people who walked alongside me on this journey.

To BookWriting.ae, thank you for your unparalleled expertise and dedication. Your belief in this story turned scattered fragments into a cohesive and meaningful narrative. The countless hours you spent refining ideas, shaping structure, and offering encouragement ensured that every word on these pages felt intentional. You reminded me, time and again, that every story is worth telling and for that, I am forever grateful.

To my therapist, whose compassion, understanding, and patience provided a safe space for me to heal. You helped me untangle the complexities of my emotions, offering clarity in moments of doubt and strength in moments of vulnerability. Your wisdom and guidance gave me the courage to embrace my journey with an open heart, transforming pain into growth and scars into wisdom.

To my family, the unshakable foundation of my life: thank you for your unwavering belief in me. To my parents, whose sacrifices taught me resilience and whose love remains my guiding light. To my siblings, for your laughter, insight, and endless reminders of the beauty in shared memories and unwavering bonds. And to my friends, who stood by me when the days felt heavy, lifting me with your encouragement and belief that I was capable of more than I could see myself.

To those who unknowingly inspired this story through their own journeys, thank you for reminding me of the universal nature of struggle and triumph. Your courage, whether directly or indirectly, helped shape the heart of this narrative.

Lastly, to my readers, thank you for opening this book and stepping into this journey with me. It is through stories, both shared and lived, that we connect with one another. My hope is that these pages offer you comfort, clarity, or perhaps even just a moment of reflection. Know that you are not alone in your struggles or your victories. This story is as much yours as it is mine.

This book would not exist without all of you. For that, and for everything you've given me, I am deeply and eternally grateful.

ABOUT THE AUTHOR

A storyteller at heart, he discovered his love for writing at the age of 16, finding solace in weaving words together to express the emotions and ideas he couldn't always say aloud. What began as quiet musings shared anonymously on social media grew into a profound connection with readers who found pieces of themselves in his reflections.

For him, writing was never about seeking fame or recognition; it was about creating a sanctuary for vulnerability and truth. Each story, each sentence, was an invitation for readers to pause and feel, to explore the depths of their own experiences, and to embrace the parts of themselves that they often left unspoken. Through his words, he sought to bridge the gap between isolation and connection, reminding others that shared humanity can be found even in the quietest corners of our lives.

Over the years, his journey as a writer evolved, shaped by both personal growth and the feedback of those who resonated with his work. Every comment, every message from a reader who felt seen or understood, reinforced his belief in the transformative power of storytelling. His writing is a reflection of his own journey, a testament to healing, resilience, and the courage it takes to confront life's challenges head on.

This book is more than just a collection of words; it is a piece of his soul. Through its pages, he hopes to inspire others to see their own strength, embrace the beauty in their scars, and find hope in the idea that even the most broken hearts can be whole again.

PROLOGUE

Not all stories of love are as they seem. Some begin with a spark that promises warmth but soon turns cold, leaving behind shadows of doubt and questions that echo long after the final goodbye. This is one such story a journey that begins with hope, pulls you into the depths of illusion, and emerges through the painful but necessary act of unraveling the truth.

Mathew believed he had found love. The kind of love that makes the world feel brighter, that fills the empty spaces of your life with laughter and light. The bond he shared with Lily felt real, pure, and unbreakable. But love, as he would come to learn, is not always what it seems. Beneath the surface of their seemingly perfect relationship lay a darkness he couldn't yet perceive a labyrinth of manipulation, control, and deceit carefully designed to keep him trapped.

Every smile, every gesture, every whispered promise had been a thread in a web Lily spun to bind him closer, to blind him to the cracks that would later shatter his world. What Mathew couldn't see, and what it would take years for him to understand, was how deeply he was entangled in a love that was never truly his.

This is not a fairy tale. It is not a story of perfect endings or happily ever afters. This is a story of awakening. It is a tale of the lies we tell ourselves to stay comfortable, the truths we avoid out of fear, and the strength it takes to break free when the illusion begins to crumble.

Mathew's journey is not an easy one, but it is one that transforms him in ways he could never have imagined. It is a path few dare to walk, fraught with pain and uncertainty, yet illuminated by moments of profound clarity and courage. Through his trials, he learns that the greatest strength often comes from breaking the very bonds you thought were meant to protect you.

What was the illusion? How deep did the deception run? And, more importantly, how did Mathew escape? These are the questions this story seeks to answer. But the answers are not simple, nor are they revealed easily. As you follow Mathew's footsteps, you will come to see that his story is not just his it is a mirror reflecting the experiences of many. It might even reflect your own.

This is a story about love, trust, betrayal, and the power of self discovery. It is about the truths we uncover when we dare to confront the lies that have defined us. As you turn these pages, prepare to question what you believe about love and what it means to truly let go.

The truth is often buried in the places we least expect, hidden beneath the surface of the lives we thought we knew. Mathew's journey is a reminder that even in the darkest moments, there is always a way forward and sometimes, the greatest act of love is learning to love yourself.

Chapter: 1

The Moment We Met: A Spark Ignited

―――――――《《‹ ❀ ›》》―――――――

"The best love is the kind that awakens the soul, makes us reach for more, plants fire in our hearts, and brings peace to our minds."

- Nicholas Sparks.

From a young age, Mathew had always been a dreamer, the kind of person who looked at the world with a sense of wonder. Growing up in a modest family, he learned early on that happiness wasn't about extravagance but about the small moments the smell of his mother's cooking filling their kitchen, his father watching the news as he always did every morning, and the quiet peace of a life lived simply.

Mathew's Family Dynamic

Mathew's family was his foundation, a steady presence in a world that often felt unpredictable. His parents, though modest in their lifestyle, were rich in warmth and affection. His mother, a selfless and genuine woman, had a knack for making anyone feel at home. She often cared for others more than she did for herself, and her kindness was something Mathew admired deeply.

Fridays were a sacred tradition in the household. Each week ended with a family lunch, where everyone gathered around the table to share simple, comforting meals. The aroma of roasted chicken and rice wafted through the house as Mathew, his siblings Bee and Ethan, caught up on the week's happenings.

Bee, the eldest, had a natural air of authority tempered by her sharp wit and nurturing nature. She was the one Mathew turned to for advice, her words often carrying the perfect mix of wisdom and humor. Ethan, the middle child, brought a vibrant energy to the family, and his animated storytelling was a highlight of every gathering.

After lunch, the family cleared the table and turned their living room into a hub of laughter and lighthearted competition. Monopoly, Scrabble, or charades it didn't matter what they played; the room was always alive with spirited debates over rules and bouts of uncontrollable laughter.

Movie nights capped off the day. They each took turns choosing the film, from Bee's heartfelt dramas to Ethan's action packed thrillers, while Mathew leaned toward quirky comedies. He still remembered his father wiping tears of laughter from his eyes after one particularly ridiculous film, a memory that made him smile even years later.

As time passed, the family dynamic evolved. When Ethan got married, Sunday lunches replaced Fridays to accommodate his wife's schedule. The gatherings grew livelier with the addition of Ethan's wife's nieces, who brought a whirlwind of energy to the house. Mathew loved watching his father entertain the kids with silly faces, his mother sneaking them extra desserts, and Bee teaching them dance moves in the living room.

It was only later in life that Mathew discovered another connection with his father. Mathew had begun anonymously sharing his writings on social media, keeping his creative outlet private. When he finally opened up about it to his family, his father surprised him by retrieving a weathered box from the storeroom. Inside were stacks of handwritten manuscripts and poems that his father had written but never shared.

"I used to write, too," his father said, smiling. "I just never had the courage to put them out there."

Together, they spent hours poring over the pages, sharing ideas and an unspoken bond. Writing became another thread that tied them together, adding a new layer to their already deep relationship.

The Café Encounter

The café where Mathew and Lily's paths first crossed was an inviting space, with sleek seats, concrete flooring, and a minimalistic design. A round barista counter sat in the middle of the café, bustling with activity. It was a place where the hum of conversation blended seamlessly with the faint aroma of coffee beans.

Lily sat near the window, idly stirring her Americano as she watched the world outside. Her gaze drifted to the man by the counter a figure who seemed entirely at ease, his easy smile lighting up his face as he exchanged jokes with the barista. There was something magnetic about him, a warmth that made her feel inexplicably drawn to his presence.

Mathew, unaware of her gaze, ordered his usual a strong black coffee and turned to find a seat. He paused briefly, his eyes meeting Lily's. She smiled, a small, tentative gesture, and he returned it with an equally soft acknowledgment. That single moment lingered, unspoken but heavy with possibility.

The Beginning of Conversations

Their first interaction was simple yet memorable. One day, while waiting for her coffee, Lily leaned over to the barista and asked, "Who's that guy? He seems like he belongs here."

The barista chuckled knowingly. "That's Mathew. He's a regular. Everyone around here knows him."

Encouraged by the barista's suggestion, Lily sent Mathew a friend request on social media later that day. To her relief, he accepted, and their conversations began. What started as casual chats soon became something deeper, a connection that grew with each message exchanged.

They discovered shared interests, from clothing and sneakers to childhood memories that sparked laughter and nostalgia. One evening, as they talked about their childhoods, Mathew shared a story about getting lost at a fair.

"I was convinced I'd been abandoned," he said, laughing. "Turns out, my mom was just two booths away, watching me panic."

Lily's laughter echoed through the phone. "Sounds like something that would happen to me," she said.

Their conversations weren't just exchanges of words they were windows into who they were, gradually building a connection that felt natural and unforced.

The Zoo Visit

One of their first dates was at the zoo, a place that held a special significance for Mathew. He told Lily stories about his childhood visits with his parents, how they'd stop for juice at a small shop by the beach before heading to the zoo.

As they walked through the zoo's paths, Mathew couldn't help but feel nostalgic. He showed Lily an old photo from a school trip and pointed to a boulder near the monkey exhibit. "That's me, twenty years ago," he laughed. Later, he recreated the same pose, chips in hand, as Lily snapped a photo.

For Lily, this glimpse into Mathew's past was endearing. It wasn't about the animals or the setting it was about seeing the world through Mathew's eyes, learning about the little things that made him who he was.

Tension with Lily's Social Circle

Though their connection was strong, it wasn't without challenges. Lily had a small group of close friends who initially encouraged her to pursue Mathew. But as their relationship deepened, tension began to brew.

Mathew never felt entirely comfortable around Lily's friends. Whenever they met, he sensed an unspoken judgment, a tension that hung in the air. He often left their gatherings early, finding it hard to fit in with a group that seemed to misunderstand him.

Even Lily admitted that she didn't always feel close to them. Sometimes, she would plan dates with Mathew to avoid outings with her friends, saying, "Let's do something, just us. I don't feel like going with them."

Mathew's Thoughts During the Beach Scene. The beach restaurant was quiet, save for the gentle clinking of glasses and the distant sound of waves. As Lily animatedly recounted a childhood story about getting lost at an amusement park, Mathew found himself captivated not just by her words but by the way she told them. Her eyes sparkled with emotion, her hands gesturing wildly as she described the chaos of being found.

Is this what love feels like? Mathew wondered, his chest tightening with a mix of exhilaration and vulnerability. For years, he had imagined what it would be like to find someone who truly understood him, someone who made the world feel brighter. And now, sitting across from Lily, he felt a flicker of that hope coming to life.

But beneath the warmth of the moment, a quiet voice whispered in the back of his mind. Love isn't just about moments like this, it cautioned. It's about the hard days, the choices, the compromises. Mathew pushed the thought aside, choosing instead to focus on the way Lily's laughter seemed to echo in his chest.

Chapter: 2

Adventures of the Heart
Love's Early Magic

————— ⟪≪⟩⟨≫⟫ —————

" Love is not finding someone to live with; it's finding someone you can't imagine living without."

- Rafael Ortiz.

There are moments in life that feel like magic, where the world seems to pause, and all that exists is the person standing beside you. For Mathew and Lily, every moment together felt like an exhilarating adventure into the unknown, a journey fueled by shared laughter, quiet revelations, and the undeniable chemistry that sparked between them.

Their relationship didn't grow slowly; it bloomed like wildflowers in spring, bursting with color and life. From the moment they began spending time together, each experience seemed to weave an invisible thread that pulled them closer, binding their hearts in ways they couldn't fully understand but instinctively trusted.

Discovering Lily's World

From their earliest days together, Lily had a habit of sharing pieces of herself in unexpected ways. She wasn't just someone who talked about her life; she showed it, leading Mathew through her favorite places in the city like an artist unveiling a masterpiece.

"Come with me," she'd said one sunny afternoon, grabbing his hand as they left the café. Mathew, curious but compliant, followed as Lily guided him down winding streets. They stopped at a quiet artistic district nestled just outside the city's bustling heart.

The area felt like it had been plucked from Lily's imagination, a maze of cobblestone alleys, dotted with intimate galleries and quirky cafés. Some galleries displayed paintings with bold, vivid strokes, while others showcased delicate sculptures that seemed to tell silent stories.

"This," Lily said, gesturing toward the district around them, "was my escape. Whenever life felt too overwhelming, I'd come here. I'd walk these streets for hours, letting the art and energy remind me of what I love about life."

Mathew could see her passion in the way her eyes lingered on each piece of art they passed. She didn't just walk these streets; she lived in them, soaking in their beauty like sunlight.

Later, they strolled to another of Lily's favorite places: a secluded park near a winding creek. "Whenever I needed to reconnect with myself," she said, pausing on a small wooden bridge that spanned the water, "I'd come here. It's quiet. Peaceful. The kind of place that lets you breathe."

Mathew felt the weight of those words. He wasn't just learning about her favorite spots; he was seeing glimpses of her soul.

Moments of Magic

As Mathew grew closer to Lily, he found himself mesmerized by the way she turned ordinary moments into extraordinary ones. One evening, they drove to a small, secluded beach outside the city, a spot that felt like it had been waiting for them.

The sun dipped low on the horizon, casting warm hues of orange and pink across the sky. The gentle lull of the waves provided the perfect backdrop as they walked hand in hand along the shoreline, their footprints leaving a trail behind them in the sand.

Mathew paused, turning to face Lily. "This beach," he said softly, his voice steady, "isn't just beautiful because of the view."

Lily tilted her head, her lips curving into a curious smile. "Why, then?"

He reached out to tuck a strand of hair behind her ear, his fingers lingering briefly against her cheek. "Because you're here," he said, his eyes locked on hers. "This moment, it feels like it was meant for us."

Her cheeks flushed, the pink of the sunset reflected in her skin. "You're good with words, you know that?" she teased gently.

"Only when they're true," he replied, his gaze unwavering.

Lily stepped closer, their faces just inches apart. "Then let's not waste it," she whispered, pulling him into a kiss as the waves crashed softly at their feet.

For Mathew, that evening wasn't just another date; it was a promise. A moment etched in time that reminded him of how love, when shared freely, could transform the simplest of places into something extraordinary.

Shared Rituals and Simple Joys

As their relationship deepened, Mathew and Lily built a world of shared rituals that became the fabric of their love. Weekends were often spent exploring new corners of the city or revisiting familiar spots that held sentimental value.

One of their favorite traditions was visiting local galleries, where Lily would introduce Mathew to her world of art. She had a way of explaining the meaning behind a painting or sculpture that made Mathew see it through her eyes.

"You don't just look at the colors," she'd say, gesturing at an abstract painting. "You feel them. You let them tell you a story."

Mathew wasn't an art enthusiast by nature, but he found himself captivated not just by the artwork but by the way Lily's face lit up as she spoke. For her, these moments were about more than art; they were about sharing a piece of herself.

In return, Mathew introduced Lily to his love for cars. On lazy afternoons, they would visit car dealerships or auto shows, where

Mathew's eyes would light up as he talked about the sleek designs and intricate mechanics of each vehicle.

"What's so special about this one?" Lily asked once, pointing to a classic convertible.

Mathew grinned. "It's not just the car; it's the history behind it. The stories it's carried, the places it's been. Every car has a soul, if you know how to look for it."

Lily didn't fully understand his fascination, but she loved the way he spoke with such passion and enthusiasm. It wasn't about the cars themselves; it was about the way they brought Mathew to life.

Quiet Intimacy

It wasn't always grand gestures or elaborate outings that defined their love. Sometimes, it was the quiet, unspoken moments that mattered most.

There were nights when they stayed in, curled up on the couch with a movie playing softly in the background. Mathew would absentmindedly trace circles on Lily's hand, while she leaned against him, her eyes fluttering closed.

In the mornings, he would order her favorite coffee and sandwich to her place. It wasn't about the grand gestures; it was about showing her, in the simplest ways, how much she meant to him.

And there were times when they'd sit in comfortable silence, lost in their own thoughts but connected in a way that needed no words.

Navigating Differences

But even as their love grew, challenges began to surface. Mathew noticed that while he was open about their relationship with his family, Lily was hesitant to introduce him to hers.

"It's not that I'm hiding you," she explained one evening. "I'm just… not ready. My family can be intense, and I want to make sure it's the right time."

Mathew nodded, though a part of him couldn't help but wonder if there was something more to her hesitation. Still, he trusted her, choosing to believe that time would bring clarity.

At the same time, Mathew struggled to find his place among Lily's social circle. Her friends, though friendly on the surface, often made him feel like an outsider.

"I don't think they dislike you," Lily said once, noticing his discomfort. "They just don't know you the way I do."

Even so, Mathew couldn't shake the feeling of tension whenever they were around her friends. It was one of the few cracks in their otherwise solid foundation, a reminder that even the strongest connections weren't without their challenges.

A Love Worth Fighting For

Despite the uncertainties and differences, Mathew and Lily's relationship remained something special something worth fighting for.

As the days turned into weeks and weeks into months, their bond deepened, built on a foundation of shared experiences, mutual respect, and an undeniable chemistry that neither could deny.

For Mathew, being with Lily felt like stepping into a world of endless possibilities, a place where he could be both vulnerable and strong.

And for Lily, being with Mathew meant finding someone who saw her not just for who she was but for who she could become.

Together, they faced the unknown, hand in hand, ready for whatever came next.

Chapter: 3

Shattered Trust: Breaking Free from Deception

―――――――――― ⫸⟡⟡⫷ ――――――――――

"One of the most courageous decisions you'll ever make is to finally let go of what is hurting your heart and soul."

- Brigitte Nicole.

The hardest truths to face are the ones that shatter the very foundations of what we believe. For Mathew, the discovery that his love for Lily was not what he thought it was would become one of the most painful and transformative experiences of his life. It wasn't just the heartbreak of losing someone he cared deeply for; it was the slow, agonizing realization that the person he had trusted and loved had been manipulating him all along.

In the Early Days

In the beginning, everything seemed perfect. Mathew was convinced that what he and Lily shared was real, pure, and unconditional. They laughed, shared dreams, and supported each other, or so he thought. But beneath the surface of their relationship, cracks began to form, and it was only a matter of time before those cracks turned into deep, unbridgeable chasms.

It started with subtle changes. Mathew noticed that Lily had an uncanny way of making everything about her. Whenever he wanted to plan something with his friends or family, Lily would suddenly be overwhelmed with emotions. She would cry, have anxiety attacks, and make him feel guilty for even considering spending time without her. At first, Mathew thought it was just her way of showing how much she loved him; after all, she seemed so emotionally invested in their relationship. But over time, he began to see the pattern. This wasn't love; this was control.

Missed Gatherings

One Friday evening, Mathew had been looking forward to joining his friends for a long planned game night. He hadn't seen them in weeks, and the thought of unwinding with familiar laughter felt like a breath of fresh air. But as he pulled on his jacket, ready to leave, Lily's voice broke the quiet.

"I just feel so left out when you're not around," she said softly, her eyes downcast. "I thought tonight could be just us."

Her words hung in the air, their weight pulling at him. She looked so vulnerable, her hands fidgeting in her lap as she sat on the couch. Mathew hesitated, torn between his plans and the pang of guilt settling in his chest. She had been so supportive lately, he reasoned. Couldn't he skip just this one night for her?

He sighed, pulling out his phone to text his friends: "Something came up. Can't make it tonight." He sat beside Lily, who leaned into him with a grateful smile. But as the evening wore on, the realization gnawed at him; this wasn't the first time she'd done this. And if he wasn't careful, it wouldn't be the last.

Criticism Disguised as Concern

It wasn't just missed gatherings that set off alarm bells. Over time, Lily's concern for Mathew often came disguised as subtle criticism.

"Why do you always need to spend so much time on that car project?" she would ask, her tone light but edged with something sharper. "Don't you think it's a little childish?"

Mathew loved restoring cars; it was his way of unwinding, a passion that connected him to the simpler joys of life. But Lily's words planted seeds of doubt. Was it childish? Should he be spending his time doing something more productive?

The comments came often enough that Mathew started to pull

away from the hobby he loved. He told himself it was to focus more on their relationship, but deep down, he felt a part of himself slowly fading.

Restaurant Confrontation: Mathew's Friends Intervene

The tension at the restaurant table was palpable. Mathew's friends had known him for years, and they could read the exhaustion in his eyes and the weariness in his forced smiles. After a round of drinks, Jake, his closest friend, leaned forward, breaking the strained silence.

"Mathew, you've changed," Jake said, his tone steady but tinged with concern. "We barely see you anymore. And when we do... you're not the same."

Mathew froze, his fingers tightening around his glass. Before he could respond, Lily's voice cut through the air like a whip.

"Oh, so it's my fault now?" she snapped, her gaze sharp as a blade. "Do you even know how hard he works? Maybe if you all supported him instead of judging, he wouldn't feel so torn."

The table fell silent, the weight of her words settling over them like a thick fog. Mathew felt the heat rise in his cheeks, his mind scrambling to defend her to defend himself. But as his friends exchanged uneasy glances, he felt something shift within him.

"I need some air," he muttered, standing abruptly. The cold night air hit him as he stepped outside, and for the first time, he let himself confront a hard truth: Lily wasn't just controlling; she was isolating him. The people who cared about him were drifting away, and he was letting it happen.

Mathew's First Therapy Session

Mathew sat stiffly on the couch, the faint hum of the air conditioner filling the room. Across from him, the therapist waited, her expression calm and open.

"So," she began gently, "what brings you here today?"

Mathew hesitated, his throat dry. He had rehearsed this moment in his mind for days, but now that he was here, the words felt heavy. "I don't even know where to start," he admitted, his voice barely above a whisper. "I just... I feel like I've lost myself."

As the session unfolded, memories spilled out like a flood. The arguments, the guilt, the suffocating sense of responsibility, and things he had buried for months came rushing to the surface. He recounted moments when Lily's words had cut him down, when her tears had felt like chains, when her love had seemed less like a comfort and more like a prison.

"It's not love," the therapist said gently, her words sinking into the silence. "It's control. And recognizing that is the first step toward healing."

Mathew nodded slowly, the weight of her words settling over him. For the first time in months, he felt a flicker of hope.

The Breakup: Final Confrontation

Mathew's apartment felt unusually quiet, the kind of silence that pressed heavily against his chest. He stood by the window, staring out at the city lights, the weight of the moment making his heart race. Lily sat on the couch, her hands clasped tightly in her lap, her expression shifting between confusion and desperation.

"You can't just do this," she said, her voice trembling. "We've been through so much together. I love you, Mathew. Doesn't that mean anything to you?"

Mathew turned to face her, his gaze steady but filled with sadness. "It means a lot, Lily. It always has. But this isn't love, not the kind of love that's healthy. I've given everything I can, but I've lost myself in the process."

Her tears spilled over, and she shook her head. "So, that's it? You're just giving up? After everything we've been through?"

"This isn't about giving up," he said firmly. "It's about finding myself again. I can't keep pouring everything into this and losing who I am. I need to be happy too, Lily."

For a moment, Lily said nothing. Then her expression hardened, anger flashing in her eyes. "Fine," she snapped, standing abruptly. "If that's what you want, then go. But don't expect to find anyone who loves you the way I do."

As the door slammed shut behind her, the weight on Mathew's chest began to lift. For the first time in years, he felt free.

Chapter: 4

Reclaiming Me:
The Path to Self Discovery

———————— ‹‹‹ ⟳෧☙ ⟳⟲ ››› ————————

"You yourself, as much as anybody in the entire universe,
deserve your love and affection."

- Buddha.

The morning sun filtered through Mathew's window, its warm light washing over the room and casting gentle patterns on the walls. For the first time in what felt like forever, the heaviness in his chest was beginning to lift. He stood by the counter, watching the steam rise from his coffee mug as the morning news played softly in the background a comforting hum that reminded him of home.

The world outside felt alive. He cracked open the window, letting the crisp air fill his lungs. A faint smile tugged at his lips. Today felt different. Not because the weight of the past was entirely gone, but because he was finally starting to see beyond it.

It had been weeks since he had walked away from Lily, and although the scars of their relationship still lingered, Mathew was starting to feel something he hadn't felt in a long time: free. The toxic grip that had once suffocated him had loosened, and for the first time in years, he was beginning to reclaim his life.

But healing wasn't a straight path. In the days following the breakup, Mathew had been plagued by waves of doubt and regret. There were nights when he couldn't sleep, replaying moments from their relationship over and over in his mind, questioning if he had made the right decision. The loneliness was palpable, and the silence in his apartment felt like a heavy, suffocating blanket.

Worse still were the betrayals. Lily's friends, once so friendly and welcoming, had turned against him, bombarding him with photos of Lily with another man. The first time he saw one of the pictures, it felt like a punch to the gut. It was as if Lily had moved on so easily, as though their time together had meant nothing to her. Seeing her smile in those pictures, happy and carefree with someone else, shattered Mathew's heart all over again.

In those dark moments, it was hard for him to believe that the relationship had ever been real. Had Lily always had someone waiting in the wings? Had she been planning her escape all along, making him believe the breakup was his idea so she could play the innocent victim?

Mathew was consumed with questions, doubts, and heartbreak. He began to have panic attacks, sharp, overwhelming waves of fear and sadness that left him breathless and trembling. He couldn't escape the feeling that he had been used, manipulated, and discarded. The realization that Lily may have been cheating on him the entire time gnawed at him, leaving him feeling lost, betrayed, and more alone than ever.

But one night, as he lay in bed staring at the ceiling, something inside Mathew shifted. He realized that if he continued down this path of self blame and heartache, he would never truly move on. It was time to take back his life. It was time to rediscover who he was before Lily, before the manipulation, before the heartbreak.

With a deep breath, Mathew made a decision: he would no longer let Lily's actions define him. He would no longer dwell on the past. This was his chance to rebuild to find himself again.

Spending Time with Friends and Family

Mathew's evenings had taken on a new rhythm. No longer lost in the haze of work or idle distractions, he began coming home earlier, carving out time for the people who had always been his anchors. His family, especially his eldest sister Bee, welcomed the change. Bee, with her wise and protective nature, often became the person he confided in most.

One quiet evening, Mathew found himself sitting across from Bee in the living room, the soft glow of the lamp highlighting her thoughtful expression.

"I still don't understand why it all fell apart," he admitted, his voice tinged with both confusion and lingering pain. "I gave her everything."

Bee leaned forward, her tone firm yet compassionate. "Mathew, listen to me," she began. "You didn't lose Lily; she lost you. She couldn't see how much you did for her." She paused, her gaze steady. "Do you think her workshops would be as successful today if it wasn't for your support? You gave her a foundation, and she didn't appreciate it."

Mathew's chest tightened, but there was also a strange sense of relief in hearing those words. Bee's unwavering honesty reminded him of the strength he had forgotten he possessed.

Bee wasn't the only one who noticed the shift. Mathew began making plans with his friends instead of waiting for their invitations, actively seeking out moments of connection. These gatherings, whether over coffee, games, or casual meals, became a safe space where laughter and camaraderie started to replace the shadow of his past.

Confronting His Loneliness

The loneliness still crept in at times, particularly in the quiet moments of the night when the world seemed to slow down. There were times when the silence felt unbearable, like a reminder of everything he had lost. But instead of running from it, Mathew made the conscious choice to confront it.

He began journaling his thoughts, spilling his emotions onto the pages without judgment or restraint. Writing became a form of catharsis, a way to untangle the knots in his heart and mind. Slowly, the act of putting his feelings into words gave him clarity and allowed him to process the pain. It didn't erase the loneliness, but it made it manageable, turning it into something he could understand rather than something that controlled him.

Rediscovering Old Joys

Mathew found solace not only in familiar places but also in the activities that once brought him joy. As the winter season approached, he and his friends organized a camping trip a tradition they hadn't indulged in for years. Under a star strewn sky, they pitched their tents and gathered around a roaring campfire. The smell of woodsmoke mingled with the crisp night air, and their laughter echoed through the forest.

Mathew joined in, helping to prepare food and sharing stories that had them all in stitches. As the fire crackled, he leaned back in his chair, staring up at the endless expanse of stars. The moment felt timeless, a reminder that even amidst change and loss, there were constants in life that could still bring him peace. When he wasn't camping, Mathew turned to soccer. Reconnecting with old friends over games in the park brought back a rush of adrenaline and camaraderie. The cheers, the casual competition, and the shared triumphs were reminders of the life he had been missing.

The Classic Car Project

Mathew's garage became his sanctuary, a place where he could lose himself in the steady rhythm of rebuilding his vintage car. The car, a lifelong dream, was a project that symbolized more than just a vehicle; it was a reflection of his own healing process. Every bolt tightened, every scratch buffed out, felt like a step toward reclaiming not just the car's former glory but his own.

A Quiet Epiphany at the Beach

One evening, Mathew found himself standing by the shore, the rhythmic crash of waves filling the silence. The ocean had always been a source of comfort for him, its vastness a reminder of how small his worries were in the grand scheme of things.

As he stood there, watching the sun dip below the horizon, a quiet realization washed over him. He didn't need to forget Lily to move on. Their relationship, though painful, had taught him important lessons about love, boundaries, and his own strength. Forgiveness, he realized, wasn't for Lily; it was for himself. Letting go of the resentment was the only way to truly move forward.

At that moment, with the salty breeze on his face and the sand beneath his feet, Mathew felt a sense of peace he hadn't known in years. The scars were still there, but they no longer felt like weights dragging him down. They were reminders of his resilience, proof that he had weathered the storm and come out stronger on the other side.

Chapter: 5

Strength in Scars:
Rising from the Ruins

────────── ⫷ ⫸ ──────────

"Out of suffering have emerged the strongest souls; the
most massive characters are seared with scars."

- Kahlil Gibran.

Mathew never imagined that love could unravel so painfully, leaving him standing amidst the wreckage of something that once seemed so beautiful. One moment, he had been planning a future with Lily, filled with hope, happiness, and shared dreams. The next, it felt like the ground had crumbled beneath him, leaving nothing but confusion, betrayal, and a profound sense of loss.

After the breakup, Mathew was left grappling with the aftermath of what had happened. How could someone who had claimed to love him suddenly feel like a stranger? How could the person he had trusted most in the world be the very source of his pain? These questions haunted him, even as he tried to rebuild his life.

But the truth was undeniable. The relationship with Lily had not just been flawed; it had been toxic, slowly eroding his sense of self until he barely recognized the man he had become. The more Mathew reflected on their time together, the more he saw how Lily's manipulations had shaped him into someone who doubted his worth and questioned his every decision. She had kept him emotionally trapped, and only now, in the aftermath, could he see how much of his freedom had been lost in the process.

Reflecting on Lily's Actions

Mathew spent countless evenings revisiting the patterns that had defined his relationship with Lily. Sometimes it was a casual comment, a small anecdote, or an observation from a friend that would trigger a memory, leading him down a path of reflection.

One night, while flipping through old photos on his phone, Mathew stumbled across an image of a dinner party they had attended together. He remembered the laughter, the clinking of glasses, and Lily's charm as she captivated the room. But now, looking back, he saw it differently how her charm often masked subtle digs at him, jokes that always seemed to land a little too close to home. She'd laugh it off, and so would everyone else, but Mathew could now see how those moments had chipped away at his confidence.

It was during one of his journaling sessions that Mathew found clarity: "Love shouldn't leave you doubting yourself. It should lift you, not diminish you." Writing it down felt like a revelation, as though he was beginning to reclaim the parts of himself he had lost.

Setting Boundaries with Friends

The aftermath of the breakup wasn't just about letting go of Lily; it was about redefining his relationships with the people in his life. Some friends unintentionally reopened old wounds, unaware of how deeply the relationship had impacted him.

One evening, Mathew joined a group dinner with mutual friends. The atmosphere was lighthearted until someone casually mentioned Lily's latest escapades, accompanied by a photo of her with her new partner. The image caught him off guard, but this time, he didn't retreat into silence. Instead, he calmly set his boundary.

"Can we change the subject?" he asked, his voice steady but firm. "I've moved on from that chapter, and I'd rather focus on what's ahead."

Though the moment felt vulnerable, it was empowering. Setting boundaries wasn't just about avoiding discomfort; it was about protecting his peace. Over time, his friends came to respect those boundaries, becoming a support system that encouraged his healing rather than hindering it.

A Symbol of Healing: The Restored Car

Mathew's garage became his sanctuary, where he poured his energy into restoring the classic car he had bought. The car wasn't just a project; it was a mirror of Mathew's healing. Every part he polished, replaced, or tightened felt symbolic, each step mirroring the internal work he was doing to rebuild himself.

One afternoon, as he struggled with a particularly stubborn bolt, Mathew smiled to himself. Nothing worth fixing happens overnight, he thought, gripping the wrench tighter. Frustration gave way to determination, and when the bolt finally gave way, it felt like a small but meaningful victory.

By the time the car neared completion, its polished exterior gleamed under the garage lights, a tangible reminder of how far he had come. "This is more than just a car," he murmured one evening, running a hand along the hood. "This is proof that broken things can be beautiful again."

Facing the Fear of New Relationships

Despite his progress, Mathew couldn't ignore the hesitation that surfaced whenever he thought about dating again. It wasn't the idea of meeting someone new that scared him; it was the thought of falling into old patterns. What if I miss the red flags again? What if history repeats itself?

In therapy, he voiced these concerns.

"I don't know if I can trust myself to get it right next time," he admitted.

"It's not about being perfect," his therapist reassured him. "It's about recognizing the signs and trusting that you now have the tools to protect your heart. You've grown, Mathew. Trust that growth."

The words resonated deeply, offering Mathew a sense of reassurance he hadn't felt in years. He didn't have to rush. Trusting himself again would take time, and that was okay.

A Quiet Triumph

One evening, Mathew decided to drive along the coast. The wind rushed through the open windows, carrying the scent of salt and freedom. For the first time in months, he felt truly at peace.

It wasn't the loud, celebratory kind of triumph he had imagined; it was quieter and more profound. The road ahead was still uncertain, but for the first time, he felt ready to face it. Not because he had everything figured out, but because he had found his strength again.

Stopping at a scenic overlook, Mathew parked the car and stepped out to take in the view. The waves crashed below, their rhythm steady and unchanging, a stark contrast to the chaos he had endured. As he leaned against the hood of his car, a small smile tugged at his lips. He thought about the man he had been at the start of this journey, unsure, hesitant, and burdened by doubt. That man felt like a distant memory now.

Closing Reflection

With each passing day, Mathew grew more certain of who he was and what he wanted out of life. He wasn't looking for validation from others anymore. Instead, he was focused on pursuing his dreams, building a life that was truly his own. Whether it was completing the restoration of his beloved car, writing more, or setting new goals for his career, Mathew was driven by a newfound passion.

The relationship with Lily had left its scars, but Mathew no longer saw those scars as something to hide. They were a part of his story, a reminder of his resilience. He had emerged from the pain stronger, more self aware, and more determined than ever to live a life that was true to who he was.

In the end, Mathew's journey wasn't just about escaping a toxic relationship it was about reclaiming his power, his identity, and his happiness. He had learned to value himself in ways he never had before, to trust his instincts, and to believe that he was worthy of love real love, the kind that wasn't built on control or manipulation.

Looking back, Mathew no longer saw his time with Lily as the end of something but rather as the beginning of something far more important: his own journey toward self empowerment. And now, standing on the other side of the storm, he knew that whatever challenges lay ahead, he was ready to face them with strength, with confidence, and with an unshakable belief in himself.

Chapter: 6

The Power of Letting Go: Finding Peace and Closure

⫷ ⟶⟵ ⫸

"Sometimes good things fall apart so better things can fall together."

- Marilyn Monroe.

Months had passed since Mathew's world had crumbled, and though the pain of his breakup with Lily still echoed in his heart, it had also set him on a path of self discovery and healing. The turbulent storm of emotions that had once gripped him had slowly given way to clarity. Now, standing on the edge of a new chapter, Mathew felt something he hadn't allowed himself to feel in a long time: hope.

A New Dawn: Reflections on Healing

The love he had once believed was unconditional had, in reality, been laced with manipulation. Therapy helped Mathew see that the relationship had been toxic long before it ended. One session, in particular, stayed with him.

"You're holding onto the guilt because it feels easier than facing the truth," his therapist said gently. "But you're not responsible for someone else's happiness. What do you gain by blaming yourself?"

The question lingered in Mathew's mind for days. One evening, as he sifted through a box of old keepsakes, he found a jacket

Lily had gifted him. It felt heavy in his hands, both physically and emotionally. He realized it was a symbol of the control she had over him the way she had intertwined her presence into every part of his life. Without hesitation, he folded the jacket and placed it into a donation box, watching it disappear into a bin filled with other discarded items.

That small act felt monumental. It wasn't just about letting go of an object but releasing the emotional chains that had bound him. He no longer needed to carry the weight of their past.

Moving to a New City: The Power of Change

The decision to move was daunting, but Mathew knew it was necessary. The day he arrived in the city felt like stepping into another world. The bustling streets hummed with life, vibrant and full of opportunity. The change felt overwhelming at first, but Mathew welcomed the challenge.

In his quiet moments, he began exploring his surroundings. Parks filled with golden leaves in the autumn, cozy cafés tucked into corners, and long walks by the river became his routine. The city had its own pulse, one that seemed to synchronize with his newfound energy.

The move wasn't just about escaping the memories of Lily it was about creating something entirely his own. Bit by bit, Mathew felt himself growing into this new version of himself, untethered from the shadows of his past.

Rebuilding from Scratch: The Classic Car Project

The car was more than just a project it had become a symbol of Mathew's resilience. As he worked on the finishing touches, polishing the chrome and adjusting the engine, he felt an immense sense of pride.

One afternoon, he decided to take the car for a drive along the coastal highway. The open road stretched before him, the sun casting a golden glow over the cliffs and ocean below. With the windows down and the wind rushing through, Mathew felt the kind of freedom he hadn't known in years.

He pulled over at a scenic lookout, stepping out to admire the view. The car gleamed in the sunlight, a testament to the effort he had poured into rebuilding it. "We did it," he murmured, running a hand along the hood. In that moment, he wasn't just looking at a restored car he was seeing a reflection of himself.

Letting Go of the Past: A Quiet Epiphany

As the sun dipped below the horizon one evening, Mathew sat on the beach, his feet buried in the cool sand. The rhythmic crash of waves felt soothing, like a lullaby for his soul.

He picked up a small stick and began tracing patterns in the sand, letting his thoughts flow freely. He wrote a single word: "Forgiveness."

The ocean's tide crept closer, washing over the letters and erasing them with a gentle sweep. Mathew smiled, watching as the word dissolved into the sea. It was a fitting metaphor letting go didn't mean forgetting; it meant accepting.

That evening, he left the beach lighter than he had felt in years, the sound of the waves echoing in his mind as a reminder that life, like the ocean, was always moving forward.

Writing as a Way Forward

In his new apartment, Mathew found solace in writing. Late at night, with the city lights twinkling outside his window, he would pour his thoughts onto the page. At first, the words came hesitantly, fragments of memories and emotions. But as the weeks passed, they began to take shape, forming a narrative of his journey.

The idea of writing a book took hold. "What if my story could help someone else?" he wondered. It wasn't about dwelling on the pain but transforming it into something meaningful. Each chapter he outlined became a step toward closure, a testament to his resilience and growth.

The Power of Forgiveness

Forgiveness didn't come easily, but it came. Mathew started by forgiving Lily not because she deserved it but because he needed to release the anger that had anchored him to the past. He wrote a letter to her, one he never intended to send, detailing his feelings and his decision to let go.

Then came the harder part: forgiving himself. He reflected on the choices he had made, the red flags he had ignored, and the times he had stayed when he should have walked away. "You did the best you could," he told himself.

Embracing the Present

Now, standing on his apartment balcony, Mathew looked out at the city skyline, a steaming mug of tea warming his hands. The journey hadn't been easy, but it had been worth it. He no longer clung to the pain of the past or feared the uncertainty of the future.

Each scar told a story, not of defeat but of survival. They were reminders of where he had been and how far he had come.

For the first time in years, Mathew felt whole, not because of anyone else, but because he had found strength within himself. As the city buzzed with life below, Mathew took a deep breath, feeling a quiet anticipation for the future. Whatever lay ahead, he was ready.

Epilogue

"Some chapters end not with finality but with a quiet strength that readies us for whatever lies ahead."

Mathew sat on the edge of his couch, the soft fabric comforting against his back as he gazed out through the floor to ceiling windows of his new apartment. The city stretched out before him, alive with twinkling lights and the murmur of distant life. Tonight, the air felt especially crisp, carrying with it the scent of possibility.

It had been months since he had left the weight of his past behind, but tonight, he could feel how much lighter he had become. Each day of his journey had been marked by small triumphs and quiet realizations, building to this very moment.

Finding Freedom

He thought back to those restless nights not so long ago when questions had filled his mind like a storm. Back then, he had replayed every word, every action, every decision, trying to piece together answers that never came. Now, the storm had passed. Mathew no longer sought closure from anyone else. He had found it within himself. The questions that once consumed him had faded into irrelevance, their sharp edges dulled by time and self reflection. It wasn't about why things had happened or how they could have been different. It was about learning, growing, and moving forward.

He took a sip from his cup of green tea, a habit he'd picked up recently, one that felt grounding. Each sip was a reminder to stay in the present, to savor the small joys that made life meaningful.

Embracing New Beginnings

The life Mathew had built here wasn't extravagant, but it was his. He spent his mornings journaling by the window, letting the golden hues of sunrise fill the room. Afternoons were a time for exploration, wandering the streets and discovering hidden courtyards, quaint bookstores, and small cafés that felt like they belonged to him alone.

His evenings, though quieter, were just as fulfilling. Sometimes he'd sit at his desk, writing chapters for his book, the pages steadily growing into a story that felt like a testament to his journey. Other times, he'd step outside for a walk, letting the cool air clear his mind as he took in the energy of the city.

Strength in Solitude

Solitude no longer felt like loneliness. Instead, it had become a time for reflection, a space to connect with himself. Mathew found joy in the little things the sound of rain against his window, the comfort of a favorite playlist, the satisfaction of cooking a meal from scratch.

There was a time when being alone had felt suffocating, a reminder of all he thought he had lost. But now, solitude was his sanctuary. It was a place where he could breathe, dream, and simply be.

A New Chapter

Mathew's journey had also reignited old dreams, ones he had once shelved in the chaos of life. Writing had become a cornerstone of his healing, and now, his book was taking shape as a story that blended honesty with hope. It wasn't just for others; it was for him. Every chapter felt like a milestone, a way to honor the path he had walked and the man he had become.

He was also planning his next adventure. The thought of traveling again filled him with a quiet excitement. Whether it was wandering the historic streets of Prague or watching the Northern Lights in Iceland, the world felt like it was opening its arms to him.

Ready for the Future

As Mathew strolled through the city streets later that night, the cool breeze brushed against his face, carrying the faint aroma of roasted chestnuts from a nearby vendor. The pavement glistened under the streetlights, reflecting the world in a kaleidoscope of colors.

He no longer feared the unknown. The road ahead wasn't entirely clear, but that was what made it exciting. Each step he took felt deliberate and confident, rooted in the strength he had built over time.

Mathew had learned to embrace his scars, not as marks of failure but as symbols of resilience. They told a story of survival, of growth, of rediscovering who he was and what he wanted from life.

As he rounded a corner, he paused to admire a small fountain in the square. The water cascaded in steady ripples, its movement calm yet purposeful. Much like his journey, it was an ongoing, ever evolving flow.

Standing there, Mathew allowed himself a smile, not because he had reached a destination but because he was finally at peace with the journey. The past no longer weighed him down, and the future no longer felt daunting. He was here, fully present, ready to embrace whatever came next.

And for the first time in a long while, Mathew felt something he hadn't allowed himself to feel before: a quiet, unshakable joy.

www.ingramcontent.com/pod-product-compliance
Lightning Source LLC
Chambersburg PA
CBHW070057100426
42740CB00013B/2862